R.I.P. Emma Lou Briggs, a play in one act by Dot Hatfield, directed by Lana Hallmark, was presented at Performing Arts Center on the Square in Searcy, Arkansas, July 15, 2011, with the following cast of characters:

Diane   Carolyn McNamee

Nikki   Madison Kuebler

Karen   Shelly White

JoEllen   Suzanne Guymon

Hal   J.R. Thomas

Suggested music:

Fill the World With Love
Music and Lyrics: Leslie Bricusse

Tapestry
Music and Lyrics: Carole King

R.I.P. Emma Lou Briggs

CAST:

DIANE   the oldest of Emma Lou's three daughters

NIKKI   DIANE'S daughter

KAREN   Emma Lou's second daughter

HAL   KAREN'S husband

JOELLEN   youngest of the three sisters

SETTING:

A small town in middle Tennessee. The action takes place in Emma Lou's living room, decorated in a style that could best be described as eclectic. A seventies-era couch and chair, bentwood rocker, antique china cabinet, console TV with rabbit ears, and a bookcase full of books. Along the wall stage left, is a portable stereo from the eighties and a stack of records. In the corner stage right, a small computer sits on a formica-top table. A door stage left leads to Emma Lou's bedroom. Center stage right is a door leading outside to the front porch.

TIME:

June, 2001, the day after Emma Lou Briggs' funeral. The song "Fill the World With Love" is heard in the background. *"Did I fill the world with love my whole life through..."*

> *(Lights up on empty stage. A key rattles in the lock and DIANE and NIKKI enter from outside.)*

NIKKI:

What's that smell?

DIANE:

It's just a little muggy in here. Turn on the air conditioner. Flip on the ceiling fan. Open the window.

NIKKI:

Which of those things do you want me to do?

DIANE:

All three.

NIKKI:

Why did Gram always keep the house so stuffy?

> *(SHE flips on fan and adjusts air conditioner. DIANE moves around the room 'straightening' things.)*

DIANE:
Oh, she didn't mean to. It's just that the last few years she was always cold. Blood gets thinner with age, you know.

NIKKI:
Yeah, I guess so. *(Sits on the couch.)* It was a nice service, Mom. What was that song the lady sang ... from the old movie? I liked that.

DIANE:
"Fill the world with love..." Petula Clark sang it in *Goodbye Mr. Chips.*" It was always one of Mom's favorites. I think it said a lot about her life, so I wanted to use it.

NIKKI:
She was a sweetie, all right. I should have come around more often, I guess, but ...

DIANE:
She knew you were busy. She always wanted to know the latest news about you. That's why she bought that second-hand computer ... so she could get email from her grandkids.

NIKKI:

Now you're making me feel guilty. I'm sorry I didn't write her more often … or come see her. But I feel kinda creepy around old people. I don't know what to say …

DIANE:

I hope you outgrow that sometime in the next thirty or forty years.

NIKKI:

Touché. Enough of that. What happened to all of Papa's stuff when he died?

DIANE:

Gosh, that was twenty years ago. Mama eventually gave his clothes to Goodwill. Kept his wedding suit, I think. It's probably still hanging in one of the upstairs closets. She drove the car till it fell apart. A couple of years ago she gave each of us something sentimental. We drew straws for wedding band, Kiwanis pin, Masonic ring – things like that. Who knows? When we look around, we might find more things of his she couldn't bear to part with.

NIKKI:

Twenty years ago. I guess Gram was pretty young to be a widow.

DIANE:

She was. We weren't sure how she would manage. My daddy was head of the household. Not mean or anything, but he made all the decisions. She went along with everything he wanted. That's the way it was back then. If she ever complained, I never heard of it. We wondered what would happen when a decision needed to be made and Daddy wasn't here to make it.

NIKKI:

So what happened?

DIANE:

She surprised us all. They had gotten married Mama's senior year in college. Then when JoEllen was old enough to start school, Mama asked Daddy about getting her teaching certificate. He said it was okay by him, so she did. She was just made for teaching. She loved it. And kids loved her.

NIKKI:

She asked his permission? What if he had said no?

DIANE:

If Daddy hadn't wanted her to work, she would have stayed a housewife.

(DIANE has pulled an old high school yearbook from the bookcase and shows it to NIKKI.)

NIKKI:

Look at that girl's hair! *(Laughing)*

DIANE:

Kinda flat on top, huh?

NIKKI:

Yeah, but the boys made up for it. What is that hairdo called?

DIANE:

That is a pompadour.

NIKKI:

Held in place with a quart of grease. (SHE flips a few pages) So when Papa died, she had the teaching job to fall back on.

DIANE:

Yes, but like I said she surprised us by deciding to go back to school and get her Masters. Hadn't set foot on a college campus for 30 years but she set her head to do it and she did.

NIKKI:
(*Smiling*) Without Papa saying it was okay?

DIANE:
I wondered at the time what he would have thought of it. Wonder if he'd have given permission if he were alive.

NIKKI:
Or if it was something she always wanted to do and couldn't.

DIANE:
Right. Then when the old car finally died, Mama was faced with having to buy another. Daddy had always bought the cars. He's just drive it home – usually surprising Mama with it.

NIKKI:
She never helped pick it out?

DIANE:
Nope. And she had no idea about the bargaining and trading. How the car dealers ask one price and you're supposed to haggle with them to get the price down. Daddy loved that sort of thing, rose to the challenge. Mama didn't have a clue.

11

NIKKI:

So what did she do?

DIANE:

Like any good teacher, she did her homework. She looked up makes and models and prices. This was before the internet, remember. She collared a salesman on one of the lots and got a lot of information from him. Then she figured out how much she should pay and how much interest.

NIKKI:

So how could she know if she was getting a lemon?

DIANE:

Well, she knew she couldn't afford a new car and it's hard to determine when a used car is in good shape, so she went to the Hertz Used Car place in Nashville. They put a sticker on the car – no haggling. And all the history of the car is an open book. So she just picked one out, called her bank and made the deal. She drove that Taurus for ten years.

NIKKI:

That's a great story, Mom. Did Gram ever think about getting married again?

DIANE:

Not that I know of. Mr. Billingsley took her out to dinner a few times but I think they were just friends.

NIKKI:

That's something I would like to know more about. You know, Mom, I wonder how often that will happen.

DIANE:

What?

NIKKI:

That something will come to mind I wish I had asked Gram about. She was so smart and had a wonderful memory. I loved her stories when I was little and now when I think of the tales she told, I want to ask more questions, clarify points, get names. Now it's too late.

> *(NIKKI rises and circles the room, peering in the china cabinet, looking at the pictures, books, etc.)*

When do the rest of them get here?

DIANE:

Anytime now, I guess. Karen and Hal are picking up JoEllen.

NIKKI:

Uncle Hal's coming?

DIANE:

Don't start.

NIKKI:

What about the twins?

DIANE:

They left this morning for cheerleading camp. A day late because of the funeral. George took them down. That's why JoEllen is coming with Karen and Hal.

(NIKKI scans the record collection near the stereo.)

NIKKI:

Look at these old LPs. Did Gram play them anymore?

DIANE:

I'm not sure the stereo even works.

NIKKI:

Here's that movie album – *"Goodbye Mr. Chips – 1960."* … a forty-year-old record.

(SHE continues to flip through album covers.)

Oh, my gosh. Here's Carole King's *Tapestry* album.
That's a classic. Mom! On the back Gram wrote "from
Di, Christmas 1972." You gave this to her! Did Gram
like Carole King?

DIANE:
I guess so. Actually, those were all my favorite songs. I
bought that for her when I was in college. I nearly wore
it thin, I loved it so.

NIKKI:
Well, they say a thoughtful gift is something *you* like.

DIANE:
Doesn't seem so thoughtful, now. To tell the truth, it
feels a little selfish. Like I didn't think of what she might
want for Christmas. I did it for myself.

NIKKI:
Knowing Gram, she loved this. (SHE moves over to the
bookcase.)

Wow! That's a bunch of books. Gram must have kept
every one she ever read.

DIANE:

No, impossible. But probably every one that was a gift. She never threw away or recycled a gift. If it wasn't used up, like food or hand lotion, it's still here somewhere.

NIKKI:

Hey, look. You're right. *(Reading from book.)* "Listen to the *Warm,* poems by Rod McKuen."

DIANE:

Oh my gosh.

NIKKI:

It says, "from Karen, 1975. Mom, hope you love this as much as I do." *(SHE randomly reads aloud from the book, laughing.)* So, what do you think? Did Gram like this poetry?

DIANE:

(Laughing.) She probably preferred Helen Steiner Rice. But I imagine she loved the gift because Karen chose it. And it gave her an idea about what Karen liked.

> *(KAREN enters, followed by her husband, HAL, and her sister, JOELLEN. All three are dressed casually but it's clear that KAREN'S outfit came from an upscale shop. HAL wears shorts and a golf shirt.)*

KAREN:
Did I hear my name mentioned?

DIANE:
Hi. Nikki found an old book you gave Mom.

KAREN:
I wouldn't be surprised. She never threw anything away.

HAL:
Okay. Let's get started. We want to leave first thing tomorrow.

DIANE:
Well, this is something we need to take care of. It may take awhile and I don't want to rush through it.

HAL:
Listen, Di … (HE shrugs.) Okay, I think I'll pull the car into the yard under the shade tree.

(HE leaves)

DIANE:
Karen, I will not be rushed through taking care of Mother's things just because Hal is on a deadline. We sisters need to do this together and he can just butt out.

17

KAREN:

No need to get all huffy. Hal has a business to run. This trip is taking money out of his pocket, you know.

DIANE:

Karen, for God's sake, our mother just died. I'm grieving about that. I need time with my sisters to deal with our loss and decide what to do with all her things.

JOELLEN:

Please, can't we do this without you two fighting? We need to agree about what's going on.

KAREN:

Well, we're going to have an estate sale, aren't we? All these antiques … that Depression Glass alone is worth a fortune.

JOELLEN:

But that belonged to Granny West, didn't it?

KAREN:

Jo, I've seen your house. You don't need any more knick-knacks collecting dust.

DIANE:

Okay. Wait. I know Mom wrote down some of her wishes. Maybe not an official will, but at least some guidelines so we can know what she wanted to happen.

JOELLEN:

That would help a lot...

DIANE:

Are you two agreeable to Nikki to take a look around Mom's room to see if she can find anything?

KAREN:

Sure, the quicker we get this settled the better.

DIANE:

Do you mind, Nikki? Just look through the desks and end tables, maybe the dresser and cedar chest. See if you can find a piece of paper that might give us an idea about what she wanted done.

NIKKI:

Sure.

>   (NIKKI goes into the bedroom as HAL comes in from
>   outside.)

HAL:

How are things coming along?

KAREN:

Nikki's looking for a will or something and we are about to discuss how to get rid of all the household items.

HAL:

An estate sale – right?

DIANE:

That's not been decided.

HAL:

Why not? It's the most sensible…

DIANE:

Not for all of us.

HAL:

Karen, I can't stay here forever. You said this wouldn't take long.

KAREN:

We have to talk through a few things first. We can do that while Nikki's looking.

(HAL pulls out his cell phone and engages in a conversation. HE eventually leaves during the following.)

DIANE:

Now, about a sale. We may need to have one eventually to clear out the last of it. But I think most of these things have sentimental value. Some of it I would like to keep, and I think Nikki would like to have a memento of her grandmother.

KAREN:

Nikki!

JOELLEN:

I think Jan and Joy would like something, too.

KAREN:

The grandchildren shouldn't even be considered in the division of things. That isn't fair to me. I don't have a child.

DIANE:

(Aside) That's debatable.

KAREN:

What was that?

JOELLEN:
Never mind. I know my girls will want a remembrance.
I'll share with them. If we each choose three items, I can
keep one and give one to each of my girls. Di will pick
three and give something to Nikki and you will have
three to do with as you please. Let's just don't fight!

KAREN:
You have to realize that everything you give your girls
cuts into my share – takes away from the profit of the
estate sale.

DIANE:
Fine by me. I don't care if we never make a cent from an
estate sale.

(NIKKI appears from the bedroom.)

NIKKI:
Did you know Gram kept a journal?

(The three women stare at her, make no response.)

NIKKI:

She did. She wrote her thoughts on current affairs, news about us, and reflections on things she read. Listen to this: "May 9, 1999. Today is Mother's Day, but no cards or calls. I know the girls are busy, but how do you forget Mother's Day? There are quite a few reminders around, after all." Then she wrote a memory about Granny West.

JOELLEN:

We all forgot Mother's Day? What year was that?

NIKKI:

1999.

JOELLEN:

I always sent something … I was probably late.

KAREN:

I don't go in for these holidays dreamed up by big business. I did things for her at other times during the year. I may have passed up Mother's Day occasionally because I don't believe in it.

DIANE:
Oh, give it a rest, Karen. I think that was the year I had been here just the week before. I guess I thought that was enough. I never thought how that might feel to her.

NIKKI:
I'd sure never get by with an excuse like that.

(DIANE scorches her with a look.)

KAREN:
Never mind all that. Nikki, if Mom kept a journal, that's the logical place to find a will.

NIKKI:
Oh … Oh … Listen to this: "Well, it's not going to happen. I thought George Billingsley was someone I could love, could enjoy growing old with. Have some companionship. But this is the end of that dream. It will never happen now. It's a little sad to think of going on alone, but there are worse things than being alone.'

JOELLEN:
What is that about?

DIANE:
You remember. She and Mr. Billingsley went out a few times.

JOELLEN:
Oh, yes. That friend of Daddy's ...

KAREN:
Really? You think they seriously talked about getting married or something?

JOELLEN:
And then didn't for some reason?

NIKKI:
Wonder what happened?

DIANE:
I don't suppose we'll ever know.

KAREN:
Maybe he was impotent. I've read a lot of articles about how seniors still enjoy sex.

(JOELLEN claps her hands over her ears. NIKKI laughs aloud. DIANE and JOELLEN speak simultaneously.)

JOELLEN:

(hands over ears) La, la, la, la, la,la

DIANE:

Karen! For Pete's sake!

KAREN:

What?

DIANE:

Well, for one thing, when Mama and Mr. Billingsley were going out she wasn't much older than I am, thank you very much.

JOELLEN:

And I don't want to talk about this!

DIANE:

Nikki, keep looking. And stop reading unless it has to do with what we're looking for. Also, I think she had one of those fire-proof boxes. It's blue … about the size of a tackle box.

(NIKKI leaves as HAL enters from the front porch.)

HAL:

Are we making any progress at all? Karen, need I remind you we have a flight tomorrow morning?

DIANE:

Hal, why don't you go ahead and go on back. Karen can stay here with us for a few days and help get this all settled.

HAL:

Karen has responsibilities, too. The Junior League is having a major fundraiser at Christmas and she is on the planning committee.

DIANE:

Junior League? Are you kidding me? Isn't that for twenty-something socialites? And Karen has to help them plan an event that's still six months away?

HAL:

As a Past President, Karen is on the advisory committee and still an active part of the organization. She connects with women whose husbands are business associates of mine. Her work with charity functions helps me tremendously.

DIANE:

It seems to me that this is important, too. Karen needs...

KAREN:

Will you two PLEASE stop talking about me as though I were on Mars? I'm right here in the same room with you and capable of speaking for myself.

JOELLEN:

Come on … Karen … Diane … please don't argue. Can't we just agree to discuss this peaceably? Where were we? Oh yes … everyone choose three things.

KAREN:

And the rest goes to an estate sale?

DIANE:

We have to go through it first.

KAREN:

There are companies that do that.

JOELLEN:

I'm with Di on this one. I hate to think of strangers pawing through Mom's stuff.

KAREN:

Oh, for Pete's sake.

HAL:

Karen's right. I think…

Praise for A Cowboy Tradition: Poems from the Heart

"Country Music created by Indian artists is in non-rhyming, four-line stanzas. It tells a simple, non-embellished story and gets done. This material strikes me as being in that style." — Review, *The Western Way*

Praise for Meadow Muffins in the Trail

"Galarneau closes this collection with two thoroughly absorbing and well-crafted short stories . . . The theme here is, as the title should suggest to you, the minor . . . and sometimes more than minor . . . adversities one is apt to encounter along the path. Step lively, and try these out for yourself." — Rick Huff, *Western Way Magazine*

RUMINATIONS
OF AN OLD WOMAN

T.K GALARNEAU

GusGus Press • Fairfield, California

978-1-945805-61-5 paperback

Cover Photo
by
T.K. Galarneau

Cover Design
by

Sappling

Studio

GusGus Press
a division of
Bedazzled Ink Publishing Company
Fairfield, California
http://gusgus.bedazzledink.com
http://www.bedazzledink.com

FOREWORD

"Youth is wasted on the young." This was dad's favorite saying, usually said to me after I'd done something without thinking and the consequences weren't favorable . . . to me or anyone else.

When we get to a certain point in our lives, some of us take time to reflect upon how far we've come and how far we've yet to go. Our own mortality rears its ugly head and we tend to panic a bit. We ask ourselves all kinds of questions: did I do right by my friends and family; did we contribute to society in some small way; or most importantly did we learn anything along the road we traveled.

Ruminations of an Old Woman is a collection of poems in which I take stock of what I learned in my life. I'm passing this wisdom along to you; I hope you gain a little knowledge from my mistakes. The lone short story, "Winston" is the tale of a young man left to his own devices at a young age. Luckily, he meets and old cowboy who helps him up the trail.

Enjoy; always remember, "Some folks live and learn and some folks just live."

CONTENTS

Part I

Part II

PART I

ALL YOU CAN OWN

I was ridin' the fence checkin' for breaks.
We lost some cows; Pa wanted 'em found.
I spent most the mornin' coverin' our range.
When not far up ahead I heard 'em bawl.

On the horizon I spied an old cow hand
Pushin' our Angus down 'long the fence
Headin' west t'ward home. Since I never
Met him that seemed a might odd.

I spurred up my pony and caught up to him
"Hey old timer," I yelled out. "Those are
Our cows, can't you see that big brand?"
I figured that'd scare him, ain't that a laugh.

That old cowpoke was singin' out low.
He chewed on his pipe as he moved along.
"Missy," he said, "I can read a brand. Your
Brand is known throughout the land."

"I'm sorry old man. Didn't want to imply
You was walkin' away with any cow hides.
'Cept my old man is madder than heck
Just mad enough to ring my neck."

I was s'posed to fix that danged old fence
'Stead I went out with somma my friends.
Parents they think work should come first
But they forget they was young once too.

"I owe you my thanks," I said as we rode
Pushin' them cows all the way back home
The buckaroo kept his thoughts to hisself
So I had to prod to just to get him to talk.

"How did ya come to the state you're in?"
As old as he was I was sure he was broke.
Not only that it appeared to me he hadn't
Kept up with the times for don't ya see.

He wore no watch, not even a ring.
I looked this old man over real good.
Needless to say he looked awful sad.
The lines on his face were deep and old.

The clothes that he wore were dirty and worn
His boots, chaps and spurs had long seen their day.
His pony and dog seemed as old as the man.
But the gleam in their eyes was sharp and keen.

The old man took his time, he explained to me
He made a list of all the things we should own.
"Wealth," he said, "ain't things we can bank.
Riches are things ya can count on one hand."

What would he know 'bout wealth or fame.
I figured this man had not a cent to his name.
"Mister you look like you seen better days.
How can wealth be found on just one hand?"

The cowpoke took a long pull on his pipe and
Blew out the smoke real slow 'fore he spoke.
"Missy," he asked, "how old might ya be?"
Proudly I said, "Just turned twenty-two."

Ruminations

"Then you haven't seen much of this ol world.
Just sit down there yonder, I'll tell you a tale."
I looked at my watch, I had somewhere to be.
"How long will this take, I'm real busy today."

"You may not believe it but once I was rich.
I had land and cattle; figured I was fixed."
"You're right old man. That's hard to believe.
Must have been foolish to lose all you owned."

"Yes sir, a fool I was, but not how you think.
What I lost weren't mere riches and fame
I lost more than things and that's what is sad."
He left me perplexed; what more could ya lose?

"Mister," I asked, "I don't understand. What
More could ya lose than all that you owned?"
"The one thing ya can't afford to lose," The cowpoke
replied. "The friends ya count on yore right hand."

I was stopped in my tracks; I had no reply.
I had dreams of wealth as yet to amass.
Did I have friends I could count on one hand?
He made me take pause and rethink my plan.

Free of this place I wanted to roam into the city
Live like a queen on a high hill overlooking the town
And have servants who'd attend to all of my needs.
Now what will I do about all the dreamin' I've done?

I sat there a lookin' at my right hand.
I made a fist and counted one by one.
Sure 'nough, there was five on one hand.
Folks who taught me to be honest and true.

I went to thank that old buckaroo
But when I looked up he was gone.
All I could see was a swirl of dust
Up the hill not ten yards from me.

I spurred up my pony; I headed for home
Would my pa believe a tale so bizarre?
Prob'ly not; so my counsel I'd keep, but
I'll never forget the wealth we can't bank.

DON'T LOOK BACK

Folks ain't the same from cradle to grave.
At the worst of times our friends can be vexin'.
When problems 'come too much to handle,
There aint no point in hangin' onto what is gone
More 'n likely it's prob'ly time to be movin' on.

There's worse things than havin' to move.
Just could be a new place is a might excitin'.
Ya meet new folks and have a change of scenery.
The critters ya move have a period of adjustment
But pretty soon they fit in as natural as can be.

Folks change o'r the years til ya just can't get along
Life's pages turned, you can't go back . . . even if ya wanted to.
Bridges get burned, the water flows on, time to be movin' on.
Won't be long and the vexation you felt will be way behind.
Ain't no point in lookin' back for the friendship that you lack.

Daddy once said, "When ya been replaced; don't look so sad,
There's better friends down the road. Just cross 'em off 'cause
They weren't true friends after all. Them's words to live by."
S'pose he's right that's for sure, it's their loss.

But don't need their drama just the same.
What's done is done, ain't crying in spilt milk;
There's light on the horizon for my ponies and me.
Matter of fact there's songs to be singin' . . .

"I'm movin' on . . . I'll soon be gone . . . I'm through with you
Too bad your blue . . . keep movin' on . . ." Hank Snow.

HAPPY BIRTHDAY GUS

All legs you were was plain to see.
A tad bit wobbly but strong indeed.
As time went on you grew and grew.
But not without peril until you knew.

To watch where you put your feet
Cause mom could hurt you toot sweet.
Sure as the world I lost track of time.
As plain as day you was really prime.

You weren't my gangly colt no more
By golly you had chrome galore.
I let you grow for one whole year
Until the vet fixed your gear.

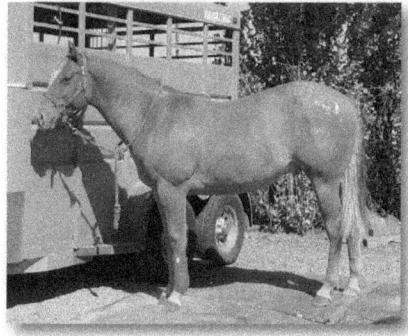

We changed your mind real dang quick.
I wanted you to listen that was the trick.
Then just for grins we wanted to see
Under saddle what you might be.

I'll be danged that saddle fit right.
Sure wouldn't be long til I sit tight.
Square in the saddle givin' the cue
To send you on; I'll be yellin' YAHOO!

I must admit I got me a dream
Of you and me being a team.
A spinnin' and a slidin' . . .
A reinin' horse a glidin'.

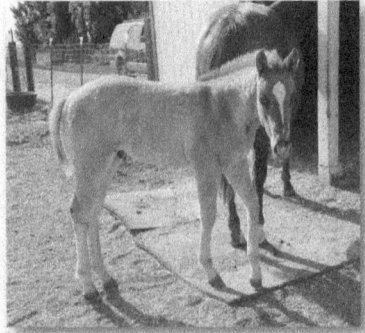

'Round the pen in a really big show.
Flaxen mane and tail all aglow.
Our friends in the stands watchin' us go.
Whoopin' and screamin', 'til I whisper whoa.

I said I was dreamin'; now I'm awake.
Dreams can come true with some give and take.
Somewhere I got a way off course.
Like puttin' the cart afore the horse.

We're celebratin' your birthday.
I'm afraid that time will slip away.
You're my bud', you're my friend.
Our whole lives we can spend.

Doin' whatever comes 'round
That sure ain't profound.
Let's look to the future in faith and hope.
'Tween us two I know we will cope.

There's a time we must part ways.
We'll go to a place to spend our days.

In joy and fun for eternity.
For now we match perfectly.

Happy birthday my friend.

HOW DO YOU KNOW

How do you know when it's time,
To saddle up and move along?

When do you know you're past your prime
And when you're a singin' your last song.

When is it time for the young folk's try
Why is it you're so damn headstrong?

The next stage of life could be so sublime
No point in draggin', no need to prolong

The clock on the wall's about to chime,
The occupation you've done lifelong

Has come to an end; no more schooltime,
The race is ending; this is the last furlong

The wind's a shiftin', could be springtime's,
Signalin' a brand new place to belong.

A body gets a hankerin' for some leisure time
To hang yer hat and play all day long.

Wait one dang minute; you ain't past your prime
All the things you're a wantin'; you're right all along

One thing's for sure, this game's got no overtime
So you and your ponies will be sayin' so long

Down any old trail; don't matter the climb
This is what you've wanted for a very long time.